Name

Address

Home | Mobile

Work | E-mail

Birthday | Anniversary

Notes

Name

Address

Home | Mobile

Work | E-mail

Birthday | Anniversary

Notes

Name

Address

Home | Mobile

Work | E-mail

Birthday | Anniversary

Notes

A

Name

Address

Home Mobile

Work E-mail

Birthday Anniversary

Notes

Name

Address

Home Mobile

Work E-mail

Birthday Anniversary

Notes

Name

Address

Home Mobile

Work E-mail

Birthday Anniversary

Notes

This

Address Book

Belongs to

Name

Address

Home | Mobile

Work | E-mail

Birthday | Anniversary

Notes

Name

Address

Home | Mobile

Work | E-mail

Birthday | Anniversary

Notes

Name

Address

Home | Mobile

Work | E-mail

Birthday | Anniversary

Notes

A

Name

Address

Home | Mobile

Work | E-mail

Birthday | Anniversary

Notes

Name

Address

Home | Mobile

Work | E-mail

Birthday | Anniversary

Notes

Name

Address

Home | Mobile

Work | E-mail

Birthday | Anniversary

Notes

Name

Address

Home Mobile

Work E-mail

Birthday Anniversary

Notes

Name

Address

Home Mobile

Work E-mail

Birthday Anniversary

Notes

Name

Address

Home Mobile

Work E-mail

Birthday Anniversary

Notes

A

Name

Address

Home Mobile

Work E-mail

Birthday Anniversary

Notes

Name

Address

Home Mobile

Work E-mail

Birthday Anniversary

Notes

Name

Address

Home Mobile

Work E-mail

Birthday Anniversary

Notes

Name

Address

Home Mobile

Work E-mail

Birthday Anniversary

Notes

Name

Address

Home Mobile

Work E-mail

Birthday Anniversary

Notes

Name

Address

Home Mobile

Work E-mail

Birthday Anniversary

Notes

B

Name

Address

Home Mobile

Work E-mail

Birthday Anniversary

Notes

Name

Address

Home Mobile

Work E-mail

Birthday Anniversary

Notes

Name

Address

Home Mobile

Work E-mail

Birthday Anniversary

Notes

Name

Address

Home Mobile

Work E-mail

Birthday Anniversary

Notes

Name

Address

Home Mobile

Work E-mail

Birthday Anniversary

Notes

Name

Address

Home Mobile

Work E-mail

Birthday Anniversary

Notes

Name

Address

Home Mobile

Work E-mail

Birthday Anniversary

Notes

Name

Address

Home Mobile

Work E-mail

Birthday Anniversary

Notes

Name

Address

Home Mobile

Work E-mail

Birthday Anniversary

Notes

Name

Address

Home Mobile

Work E-mail

Birthday Anniversary

Notes

Name

Address

Home Mobile

Work E-mail

Birthday Anniversary

Notes

Name

Address

Home Mobile

Work E-mail

Birthday Anniversary

Notes

C

Name

Address

Home | Mobile

Work | E-mail

Birthday | Anniversary

Notes

Name

Address

Home | Mobile

Work | E-mail

Birthday | Anniversary

Notes

Name

Address

Home | Mobile

Work | E-mail

Birthday | Anniversary

Notes

Name

Address

Home Mobile

Work E-mail

Birthday Anniversary

Notes

Name

Address

Home Mobile

Work E-mail

Birthday Anniversary

Notes

Name

Address

Home Mobile

Work E-mail

Birthday Anniversary

Notes

C

Name

Address

Home Mobile

Work E-mail

Birthday Anniversary

Notes

Name

Address

Home Mobile

Work E-mail

Birthday Anniversary

Notes

Name

Address

Home Mobile

Work E-mail

Birthday Anniversary

Notes

Name

Address

Home Mobile

Work E-mail

Birthday Anniversary

Notes

Name

Address

Home Mobile

Work E-mail

Birthday Anniversary

Notes

Name

Address

Home Mobile

Work E-mail

Birthday Anniversary

Notes

Name

Address

Home Mobile

Work E-mail

Birthday Anniversary

Notes

Name

Address

Home Mobile

Work E-mail

Birthday Anniversary

Notes

Name

Address

Home Mobile

Work E-mail

Birthday Anniversary

Notes

Name

Address

Home Mobile

Work E-mail

Birthday Anniversary

Notes

Name

Address

Home Mobile

Work E-mail

Birthday Anniversary

Notes

Name

Address

Home Mobile

Work E-mail

Birthday Anniversary

Notes

Name

Address

Home Mobile

Work E-mail

Birthday Anniversary

Notes

Name

Address

Home Mobile

Work E-mail

Birthday Anniversary

Notes

Name

Address

Home Mobile

Work E-mail

Birthday Anniversary

Notes

Name

Address

Home Mobile

Work E-mail

Birthday Anniversary

Notes

Name

Address

Home Mobile

Work E-mail

Birthday Anniversary

Notes

Name

Address

Home Mobile

Work E-mail

Birthday Anniversary

Notes

D

Name

Address

Home Mobile

Work E-mail

Birthday Anniversary

Notes

Name

Address

Home Mobile

Work E-mail

Birthday Anniversary

Notes

Name

Address

Home Mobile

Work E-mail

Birthday Anniversary

Notes

Name

Address

Home Mobile

Work E-mail

Birthday Anniversary

Notes

Name

Address

Home Mobile

Work E-mail

Birthday Anniversary

Notes

Name

Address

Home Mobile

Work E-mail

Birthday Anniversary

Notes

E

Name

Address

Home Mobile

Work E-mail

Birthday Anniversary

Notes

Name

Address

Home Mobile

Work E-mail

Birthday Anniversary

Notes

Name

Address

Home Mobile

Work E-mail

Birthday Anniversary

Notes

Name

Address

Home Mobile

Work E-mail

Birthday Anniversary

Notes

Name

Address

Home Mobile

Work E-mail

Birthday Anniversary

Notes

Name

Address

Home Mobile

Work E-mail

Birthday Anniversary

Notes

Name

Address

Home Mobile

Work E-mail

Birthday Anniversary

Notes

Name

Address

Home Mobile

Work E-mail

Birthday Anniversary

Notes

Name

Address

Home Mobile

Work E-mail

Birthday Anniversary

Notes

Name

Address

Home Mobile

Work E-mail

Birthday Anniversary

Notes

Name

Address

Home Mobile

Work E-mail

Birthday Anniversary

Notes

Name

Address

Home Mobile

Work E-mail

Birthday Anniversary

Notes

E

Name

Address

Home | Mobile

Work | E-mail

Birthday | Anniversary

Notes

Name

Address

Home | Mobile

Work | E-mail

Birthday | Anniversary

Notes

Name

Address

Home | Mobile

Work | E-mail

Birthday | Anniversary

Notes

Name

Address

Home Mobile

Work E-mail

Birthday Anniversary

Notes

Name

Address

Home Mobile

Work E-mail

Birthday Anniversary

Notes

Name

Address

Home Mobile

Work E-mail

Birthday Anniversary

Notes

F

Name

Address

Home Mobile

Work E-mail

Birthday Anniversary

Notes

Name

Address

Home Mobile

Work E-mail

Birthday Anniversary

Notes

Name

Address

Home Mobile

Work E-mail

Birthday Anniversary

Notes

Name

Address

Home Mobile

Work E-mail

Birthday Anniversary

Notes

Name

Address

Home Mobile

Work E-mail

Birthday Anniversary

Notes

Name

Address

Home Mobile

Work E-mail

Birthday Anniversary

Notes

Name

Address

Home Mobile

Work E-mail

Birthday Anniversary

Notes

Name

Address

Home Mobile

Work E-mail

Birthday Anniversary

Notes

Name

Address

Home Mobile

Work E-mail

Birthday Anniversary

Notes

Name

Address

Home Mobile

Work E-mail

Birthday Anniversary

Notes

Name

Address

Home Mobile

Work E-mail

Birthday Anniversary

Notes

Name

Address

Home Mobile

Work E-mail

Birthday Anniversary

Notes

G

Name

Address

Home Mobile

Work E-mail

Birthday Anniversary

Notes

Name

Address

Home Mobile

Work E-mail

Birthday Anniversary

Notes

Name

Address

Home Mobile

Work E-mail

Birthday Anniversary

Notes

Name

Address

Home Mobile

Work E-mail

Birthday Anniversary

Notes

Name

Address

Home Mobile

Work E-mail

Birthday Anniversary

Notes

Name

Address

Home Mobile

Work E-mail

Birthday Anniversary

Notes

G

Name

Address

Home | Mobile

Work | E-mail

Birthday | Anniversary

Notes

Name

Address

Home | Mobile

Work | E-mail

Birthday | Anniversary

Notes

Name

Address

Home | Mobile

Work | E-mail

Birthday | Anniversary

Notes

Name

Address

Home Mobile

Work E-mail

Birthday Anniversary

Notes

Name

Address

Home Mobile

Work E-mail

Birthday Anniversary

Notes

Name

Address

Home Mobile

Work E-mail

Birthday Anniversary

Notes

H

Name

Address

Home Mobile

Work E-mail

Birthday Anniversary

Notes

Name

Address

Home Mobile

Work E-mail

Birthday Anniversary

Notes

Name

Address

Home Mobile

Work E-mail

Birthday Anniversary

Notes

Name

Address

Home Mobile

Work E-mail

Birthday Anniversary

Notes

Name

Address

Home Mobile

Work E-mail

Birthday Anniversary

Notes

Name

Address

Home Mobile

Work E-mail

Birthday Anniversary

Notes

H

Name

Address

Home Mobile

Work E-mail

Birthday Anniversary

Notes

Name

Address

Home Mobile

Work E-mail

Birthday Anniversary

Notes

Name

Address

Home Mobile

Work E-mail

Birthday Anniversary

Notes

Name

Address

Home Mobile

Work E-mail

Birthday Anniversary

Notes

Name

Address

Home Mobile

Work E-mail

Birthday Anniversary

Notes

Name

Address

Home Mobile

Work E-mail

Birthday Anniversary

Notes

Name

Address

Home Mobile

Work E-mail

Birthday Anniversary

Notes

Name

Address

Home Mobile

Work E-mail

Birthday Anniversary

Notes

Name

Address

Home Mobile

Work E-mail

Birthday Anniversary

Notes

Name

Address

Home Mobile

Work E-mail

Birthday Anniversary

Notes

Name

Address

Home Mobile

Work E-mail

Birthday Anniversary

Notes

Name

Address

Home Mobile

Work E-mail

Birthday Anniversary

Notes

Name

Address

Home Mobile

Work E-mail

Birthday Anniversary

Notes

Name

Address

Home Mobile

Work E-mail

Birthday Anniversary

Notes

Name

Address

Home Mobile

Work E-mail

Birthday Anniversary

Notes

Name

Address

Home Mobile

Work E-mail

Birthday Anniversary

Notes

Name

Address

Home Mobile

Work E-mail

Birthday Anniversary

Notes

Name

Address

Home Mobile

Work E-mail

Birthday Anniversary

Notes

Name

Address

Home Mobile

Work E-mail

Birthday Anniversary

Notes

Name

Address

Home Mobile

Work E-mail

Birthday Anniversary

Notes

Name

Address

Home Mobile

Work E-mail

Birthday Anniversary

Notes

Name

Address

Home Mobile

Work E-mail

Birthday Anniversary

Notes

Name

Address

Home Mobile

Work E-mail

Birthday Anniversary

Notes

Name

Address

Home Mobile

Work E-mail

Birthday Anniversary

Notes

Name

Address

Home Mobile

Work E-mail

Birthday Anniversary

Notes

Name

Address

Home Mobile

Work E-mail

Birthday Anniversary

Notes

Name

Address

Home Mobile

Work E-mail

Birthday Anniversary

Notes

Name

Address

Home Mobile

Work E-mail

Birthday Anniversary

Notes

Name

Address

Home Mobile

Work E-mail

Birthday Anniversary

Notes

Name

Address

Home Mobile

Work E-mail

Birthday Anniversary

Notes

J

Name

Address

Home | Mobile

Work | E-mail

Birthday | Anniversary

Notes

Name

Address

Home | Mobile

Work | E-mail

Birthday | Anniversary

Notes

Name

Address

Home | Mobile

Work | E-mail

Birthday | Anniversary

Notes

Name

Address

Home Mobile

Work E-mail

Birthday Anniversary

Notes

Name

Address

Home Mobile

Work E-mail

Birthday Anniversary

Notes

Name

Address

Home Mobile

Work E-mail

Birthday Anniversary

Notes

K

Name

Address

Home Mobile

Work E-mail

Birthday Anniversary

Notes

Name

Address

Home Mobile

Work E-mail

Birthday Anniversary

Notes

Name

Address

Home Mobile

Work E-mail

Birthday Anniversary

Notes

Name

Address

Home Mobile

Work E-mail

Birthday Anniversary

Notes

Name

Address

Home Mobile

Work E-mail

Birthday Anniversary

Notes

Name

Address

Home Mobile

Work E-mail

Birthday Anniversary

Notes

K

Name

Address

Home Mobile

Work E-mail

Birthday Anniversary

Notes

Name

Address

Home Mobile

Work E-mail

Birthday Anniversary

Notes

Name

Address

Home Mobile

Work E-mail

Birthday Anniversary

Notes

Name

Address

Home Mobile

Work E-mail

Birthday Anniversary

Notes

Name

Address

Home Mobile

Work E-mail

Birthday Anniversary

Notes

Name

Address

Home Mobile

Work E-mail

Birthday Anniversary

Notes

K

Name

Address

Home | Mobile

Work | E-mail

Birthday | Anniversary

Notes

Name

Address

Home | Mobile

Work | E-mail

Birthday | Anniversary

Notes

Name

Address

Home | Mobile

Work | E-mail

Birthday | Anniversary

Notes

Name

Address

Home Mobile

Work E-mail

Birthday Anniversary

Notes

Name

Address

Home Mobile

Work E-mail

Birthday Anniversary

Notes

Name

Address

Home Mobile

Work E-mail

Birthday Anniversary

Notes

Name

Address

Home Mobile

Work E-mail

Birthday Anniversary

Notes

Name

Address

Home Mobile

Work E-mail

Birthday Anniversary

Notes

Name

Address

Home Mobile

Work E-mail

Birthday Anniversary

Notes

Name

Address

Home Mobile

Work E-mail

Birthday Anniversary

Notes

Name

Address

Home Mobile

Work E-mail

Birthday Anniversary

Notes

Name

Address

Home Mobile

Work E-mail

Birthday Anniversary

Notes

Name

Address

Home Mobile

Work E-mail

Birthday Anniversary

Notes

Name

Address

Home Mobile

Work E-mail

Birthday Anniversary

Notes

Name

Address

Home Mobile

Work E-mail

Birthday Anniversary

Notes

Name

Address

Home Mobile

Work E-mail

Birthday Anniversary

Notes

Name

Address

Home Mobile

Work E-mail

Birthday Anniversary

Notes

Name

Address

Home Mobile

Work E-mail

Birthday Anniversary

Notes

Name

Address

Home Mobile

Work E-mail

Birthday Anniversary

Notes

Name

Address

Home Mobile

Work E-mail

Birthday Anniversary

Notes

Name

Address

Home Mobile

Work E-mail

Birthday Anniversary

Notes

Name

Address

Home Mobile

Work E-mail

Birthday Anniversary

Notes

Name

Address

Home Mobile

Work E-mail

Birthday Anniversary

Notes

Name

Address

Home Mobile

Work E-mail

Birthday Anniversary

Notes

Name

Address

Home Mobile

Work E-mail

Birthday Anniversary

Notes

Name

Address

Home Mobile

Work E-mail

Birthday Anniversary

Notes

Name

Address

Home Mobile

Work E-mail

Birthday Anniversary

Notes

Name

Address

Home Mobile

Work E-mail

Birthday Anniversary

Notes

Name

Address

Home Mobile

Work E-mail

Birthday Anniversary

Notes

Name

Address

Home Mobile

Work E-mail

Birthday Anniversary

Notes

Name

Address

Home Mobile

Work E-mail

Birthday Anniversary

Notes

Name

Address

Home Mobile

Work E-mail

Birthday Anniversary

Notes

Name

Address

Home Mobile

Work E-mail

Birthday Anniversary

Notes

Name

Address

Home Mobile

Work E-mail

Birthday Anniversary

Notes

Name

Address

Home Mobile

Work E-mail

Birthday Anniversary

Notes

Name

Address

Home Mobile

Work E-mail

Birthday Anniversary

Notes

Name

Address

Home Mobile

Work E-mail

Birthday Anniversary

Notes

Name

Address

Home Mobile

Work E-mail

Birthday Anniversary

Notes

Name

Address

Home Mobile

Work E-mail

Birthday Anniversary

Notes

Name

Address

Home Mobile

Work E-mail

Birthday Anniversary

Notes

Name

Address

Home Mobile

Work E-mail

Birthday Anniversary

Notes

Name

Address

Home Mobile

Work E-mail

Birthday Anniversary

Notes

N

Name

Address

Home | Mobile

Work | E-mail

Birthday | Anniversary

Notes

Name

Address

Home | Mobile

Work | E-mail

Birthday | Anniversary

Notes

Name

Address

Home | Mobile

Work | E-mail

Birthday | Anniversary

Notes

Name

Address

Home Mobile

Work E-mail

Birthday Anniversary

Notes

Name

Address

Home Mobile

Work E-mail

Birthday Anniversary

Notes

Name

Address

Home Mobile

Work E-mail

Birthday Anniversary

Notes

Name

Address

Home Mobile

Work E-mail

Birthday Anniversary

Notes

Name

Address

Home Mobile

Work E-mail

Birthday Anniversary

Notes

Name

Address

Home Mobile

Work E-mail

Birthday Anniversary

Notes

Name

Address

Home Mobile

Work E-mail

Birthday Anniversary

Notes

Name

Address

Home Mobile

Work E-mail

Birthday Anniversary

Notes

Name

Address

Home Mobile

Work E-mail

Birthday Anniversary

Notes

Name

Address

Home Mobile

Work E-mail

Birthday Anniversary

Notes

Name

Address

Home Mobile

Work E-mail

Birthday Anniversary

Notes

Name

Address

Home Mobile

Work E-mail

Birthday Anniversary

Notes

Name

Address

Home Mobile

Work E-mail

Birthday Anniversary

Notes

Name

Address

Home Mobile

Work E-mail

Birthday Anniversary

Notes

Name

Address

Home Mobile

Work E-mail

Birthday Anniversary

Notes

Name

Address

Home Mobile

Work E-mail

Birthday Anniversary

Notes

Name

Address

Home Mobile

Work E-mail

Birthday Anniversary

Notes

Name

Address

Home Mobile

Work E-mail

Birthday Anniversary

Notes

Name

Address

Home Mobile

Work E-mail

Birthday Anniversary

Notes

Name

Address

Home Mobile

Work E-mail

Birthday Anniversary

Notes

Name

Address

Home Mobile

Work E-mail

Birthday Anniversary

Notes

Name

Address

Home Mobile

Work E-mail

Birthday Anniversary

Notes

Name

Address

Home Mobile

Work E-mail

Birthday Anniversary

Notes

Name

Address

Home Mobile

Work E-mail

Birthday Anniversary

Notes

Name

Address

Home Mobile

Work E-mail

Birthday Anniversary

Notes

Name

Address

Home Mobile

Work E-mail

Birthday Anniversary

Notes

Name

Address

Home Mobile

Work E-mail

Birthday Anniversary

Notes

P

Name

Address

Home Mobile

Work E-mail

Birthday Anniversary

Notes

Name

Address

Home Mobile

Work E-mail

Birthday Anniversary

Notes

Name

Address

Home Mobile

Work E-mail

Birthday Anniversary

Notes

Name

Address

Home Mobile

Work E-mail

Birthday Anniversary

Notes

Name

Address

Home Mobile

Work E-mail

Birthday Anniversary

Notes

Name

Address

Home Mobile

Work E-mail

Birthday Anniversary

Notes

Q

Name

Address

Home | Mobile

Work | E-mail

Birthday | Anniversary

Notes

Name

Address

Home | Mobile

Work | E-mail

Birthday | Anniversary

Notes

Name

Address

Home | Mobile

Work | E-mail

Birthday | Anniversary

Notes

Name

Address

Home Mobile

Work E-mail

Birthday Anniversary

Notes

Name

Address

Home Mobile

Work E-mail

Birthday Anniversary

Notes

Name

Address

Home Mobile

Work E-mail

Birthday Anniversary

Notes

R

Name

Address

Home Mobile

Work E-mail

Birthday Anniversary

Notes

Name

Address

Home Mobile

Work E-mail

Birthday Anniversary

Notes

Name

Address

Home Mobile

Work E-mail

Birthday Anniversary

Notes

Name

Address

Home Mobile

Work E-mail

Birthday Anniversary

Notes

Name

Address

Home Mobile

Work E-mail

Birthday Anniversary

Notes

Name

Address

Home Mobile

Work E-mail

Birthday Anniversary

Notes

R

Name

Address

Home Mobile

Work E-mail

Birthday Anniversary

Notes

Name

Address

Home Mobile

Work E-mail

Birthday Anniversary

Notes

Name

Address

Home Mobile

Work E-mail

Birthday Anniversary

Notes

Name

Address

Home | Mobile

Work | E-mail

Birthday | Anniversary

Notes

Name

Address

Home | Mobile

Work | E-mail

Birthday | Anniversary

Notes

Name

Address

Home | Mobile

Work | E-mail

Birthday | Anniversary

Notes

R

Name

Address

Home
Mobile

Work
E-mail

Birthday
Anniversary

Notes

Name

Address

Home
Mobile

Work
E-mail

Birthday
Anniversary

Notes

Name

Address

Home
Mobile

Work
E-mail

Birthday
Anniversary

Notes

Name

Address

Home Mobile

Work E-mail

Birthday Anniversary

Notes

Name

Address

Home Mobile

Work E-mail

Birthday Anniversary

Notes

Name

Address

Home Mobile

Work E-mail

Birthday Anniversary

Notes

Name

Address

Home Mobile

Work E-mail

Birthday Anniversary

Notes

Name

Address

Home Mobile

Work E-mail

Birthday Anniversary

Notes

Name

Address

Home Mobile

Work E-mail

Birthday Anniversary

Notes

Name

Address

Home Mobile

Work E-mail

Birthday Anniversary

Notes

Name

Address

Home Mobile

Work E-mail

Birthday Anniversary

Notes

Name

Address

Home Mobile

Work E-mail

Birthday Anniversary

Notes

S

Name

Address

Home | Mobile

Work | E-mail

Birthday | Anniversary

Notes

Name

Address

Home | Mobile

Work | E-mail

Birthday | Anniversary

Notes

Name

Address

Home | Mobile

Work | E-mail

Birthday | Anniversary

Notes

Name

Address

Home Mobile

Work E-mail

Birthday Anniversary

Notes

Name

Address

Home Mobile

Work E-mail

Birthday Anniversary

Notes

Name

Address

Home Mobile

Work E-mail

Birthday Anniversary

Notes

Name

Address

Home Mobile

Work E-mail

Birthday Anniversary

Notes

Name

Address

Home Mobile

Work E-mail

Birthday Anniversary

Notes

Name

Address

Home Mobile

Work E-mail

Birthday Anniversary

Notes

Name

Address

Home | Mobile

Work | E-mail

Birthday | Anniversary

Notes

Name

Address

Home | Mobile

Work | E-mail

Birthday | Anniversary

Notes

Name

Address

Home | Mobile

Work | E-mail

Birthday | Anniversary

Notes

T

Name

Address

Home | Mobile

Work | E-mail

Birthday | Anniversary

Notes

Name

Address

Home | Mobile

Work | E-mail

Birthday | Anniversary

Notes

Name

Address

Home | Mobile

Work | E-mail

Birthday | Anniversary

Notes

Name

Address

Home Mobile

Work E-mail

Birthday Anniversary

Notes

Name

Address

Home Mobile

Work E-mail

Birthday Anniversary

Notes

Name

Address

Home Mobile

Work E-mail

Birthday Anniversary

Notes

T

Name

Address

Home Mobile

Work E-mail

Birthday Anniversary

Notes

Name

Address

Home Mobile

Work E-mail

Birthday Anniversary

Notes

Name

Address

Home Mobile

Work E-mail

Birthday Anniversary

Notes

Name

Address

Home Mobile

Work E-mail

Birthday Anniversary

Notes

Name

Address

Home Mobile

Work E-mail

Birthday Anniversary

Notes

Name

Address

Home Mobile

Work E-mail

Birthday Anniversary

Notes

Name

Address

Home Mobile

Work E-mail

Birthday Anniversary

Notes

Name

Address

Home Mobile

Work E-mail

Birthday Anniversary

Notes

Name

Address

Home Mobile

Work E-mail

Birthday Anniversary

Notes

Name

Address

Home Mobile

Work E-mail

Birthday Anniversary

Notes

Name

Address

Home Mobile

Work E-mail

Birthday Anniversary

Notes

Name

Address

Home Mobile

Work E-mail

Birthday Anniversary

Notes

Name

Address

Home | Mobile

Work | E-mail

Birthday | Anniversary

Notes

Name

Address

Home | Mobile

Work | E-mail

Birthday | Anniversary

Notes

Name

Address

Home | Mobile

Work | E-mail

Birthday | Anniversary

Notes

Name

Address

Home Mobile

Work E-mail

Birthday Anniversary

Notes

Name

Address

Home Mobile

Work E-mail

Birthday Anniversary

Notes

Name

Address

Home Mobile

Work E-mail

Birthday Anniversary

Notes

Name

Address

Home Mobile

Work E-mail

Birthday Anniversary

Notes

Name

Address

Home Mobile

Work E-mail

Birthday Anniversary

Notes

Name

Address

Home Mobile

Work E-mail

Birthday Anniversary

Notes

Name

Address

Home | Mobile

Work | E-mail

Birthday | Anniversary

Notes

Name

Address

Home | Mobile

Work | E-mail

Birthday | Anniversary

Notes

Name

Address

Home | Mobile

Work | E-mail

Birthday | Anniversary

Notes

Name

Address

Home Mobile

Work E-mail

Birthday Anniversary

Notes

Name

Address

Home Mobile

Work E-mail

Birthday Anniversary

Notes

Name

Address

Home Mobile

Work E-mail

Birthday Anniversary

Notes

Name

Address

Home Mobile

Work E-mail

Birthday Anniversary

Notes

Name

Address

Home Mobile

Work E-mail

Birthday Anniversary

Notes

Name

Address

Home Mobile

Work E-mail

Birthday Anniversary

Notes

X

Name

Address

Home Mobile

Work E-mail

Birthday Anniversary

Notes

Name

Address

Home Mobile

Work E-mail

Birthday Anniversary

Notes

Name

Address

Home Mobile

Work E-mail

Birthday Anniversary

Notes

Name

Address

Home Mobile

Work E-mail

Birthday Anniversary

Notes

Name

Address

Home Mobile

Work E-mail

Birthday Anniversary

Notes

Name

Address

Home Mobile

Work E-mail

Birthday Anniversary

Notes

Name

Address

Home Mobile

Work E-mail

Birthday Anniversary

Notes

Name

Address

Home Mobile

Work E-mail

Birthday Anniversary

Notes

Name

Address

Home Mobile

Work E-mail

Birthday Anniversary

Notes

Name

Address

Home Mobile

Work E-mail

Birthday Anniversary

Notes

Name

Address

Home Mobile

Work E-mail

Birthday Anniversary

Notes

Name

Address

Home Mobile

Work E-mail

Birthday Anniversary

Notes

Name

Address

Home Mobile

Work E-mail

Birthday Anniversary

Notes

Name

Address

Home Mobile

Work E-mail

Birthday Anniversary

Notes

Name

Address

Home Mobile

Work E-mail

Birthday Anniversary

Notes

Name

Address

Home Mobile

Work E-mail

Birthday Anniversary

Notes

Name

Address

Home Mobile

Work E-mail

Birthday Anniversary

Notes

Name

Address

Home Mobile

Work E-mail

Birthday Anniversary

Notes

Name

Address

Home Mobile

Work E-mail

Birthday Anniversary

Notes

Name

Address

Home Mobile

Work E-mail

Birthday Anniversary

Notes

Name

Address

Home Mobile

Work E-mail

Birthday Anniversary

Notes

NOTES

NOTES

NOTES

NOTES

Made in the USA
Las Vegas, NV
16 May 2024